KABOOM!

A VOLCANO ERUPTS

Written by Jessica Kulekjian

Illustrated by Zoe Si

Kids Can Press

I am a volcano.

A
quiet,
slumbering
volcano.

I've been asleep for thousands of years,
but now something's stirring deep inside.

7000 YEARS AGO

5000 YEARS AGO

2000 YEARS AGO

TODAY

It looks peaceful, but its insides are heating up. It's reawakening.

A little whisper hisses through my magma chamber.

Then, gases gurgle. Steam spits out.

I sputter,

spurt

and growl.

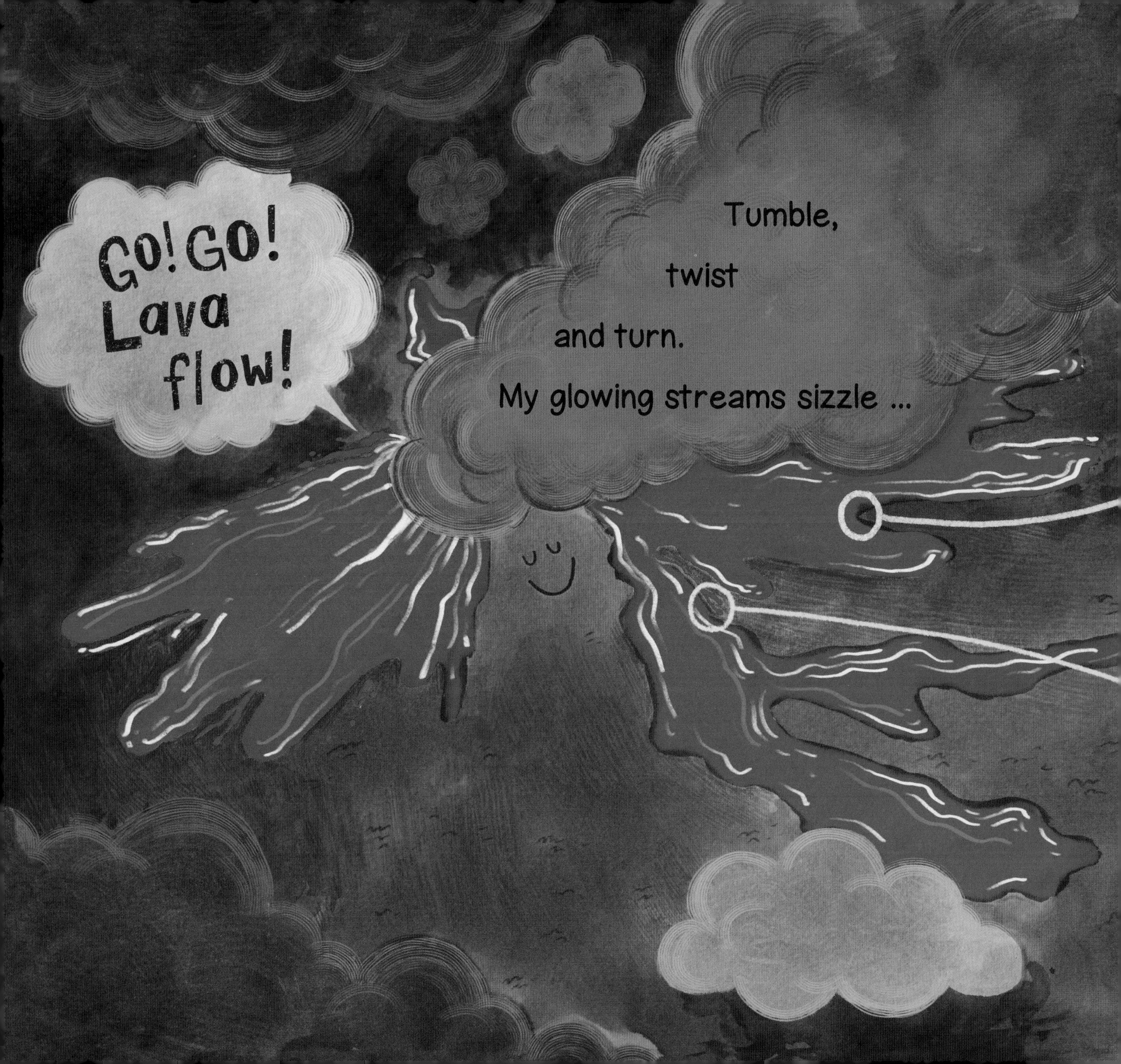

Tumble,

twist

and turn.

My glowing streams sizzle ...

then s l o w l y

cool

their

burn.

yawn

Don't touch it — yet! As
lava flows, it loses heat.
When it cools enough, it
turns back into solid rock.

I settle to a stop.

But look ...

something new begins.

Where lava once flowed, new land can form. Sometimes it creates an entirely new island! Where ash once fell, soil becomes rich with minerals, and fresh life springs up and thrives.

Now, I'm just a quiet, slumbering volcano until ...

PHASES OF VOLCANOES

Active volcanoes have erupted recently or are close to erupting again. Signs include a full magma chamber, high temperatures outside and inside the volcano and water vapor, rocks, ash or lava coming out.

Dormant volcanoes have not erupted for hundreds or even thousands of years. They can sometimes produce earthquakes or tremors, but they usually stay slumbering for long periods of time. They are still connected to their magma chambers, so it's possible they could wake up again.

Extinct volcanoes have been inactive for thousands of years. They are not connected to their magma chambers and are not expected to erupt ever again.

ANATOMY OF A VOLCANO

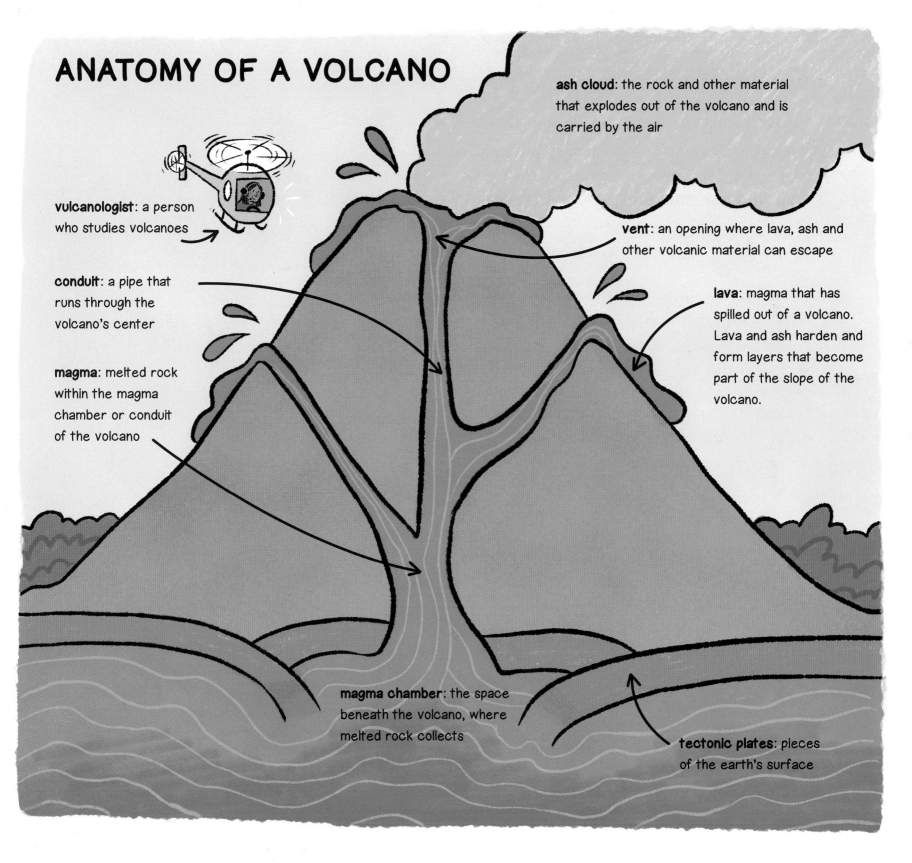

ash cloud: the rock and other material that explodes out of the volcano and is carried by the air

vulcanologist: a person who studies volcanoes

vent: an opening where lava, ash and other volcanic material can escape

conduit: a pipe that runs through the volcano's center

lava: magma that has spilled out of a volcano. Lava and ash harden and form layers that become part of the slope of the volcano.

magma: melted rock within the magma chamber or conduit of the volcano

magma chamber: the space beneath the volcano, where melted rock collects

tectonic plates: pieces of the earth's surface

COMMON TYPES OF VOLCANOES

Calderas are bowl-like structures formed by the collapse of previous volcanoes after magma has been released. Often, calderas become lakes after years of filling up with rain and snow. Crater Lake in Oregon is an example of a caldera.

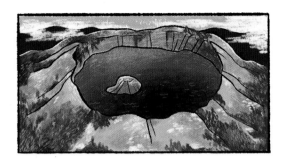

Cinder cones are the smallest volcanoes. They are created from lava that erupts, hardens and builds up over time. Cinder cones are commonly found near other volcanoes. A famous example of a cinder cone volcano is Paricutín, in Mexico. This volcano grew over several days right out of a cornfield!

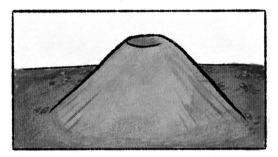

Composite volcanoes are also called **stratovolcanoes**. They look like steep mountains with a crater at the summit. Some of the most beautiful and well-known composite volcanoes include Mount Saint Helens and Mount Rainier in Washington, Mount Shasta in California, Mount Fuji in Japan and Arenal Volcano in Costa Rica (it inspired the art in this book!).

Shield volcanoes are created from liquid lava flows that spill from a vent or group of vents. Shield volcanoes don't reach the same heights as composite volcanoes. Instead, they can spread out over a large area. The Hawaiian Islands are created out of a chain of these types of volcanoes, including one of the world's largest shield volcanoes, Mauna Loa.

Submarine volcanoes form along tectonic plates on the ocean floor. About 80 percent of volcanic eruptions on Earth happen underwater! Some examples of submarine volcanoes include West Mata and Hunga Tonga-Hunga Ha'apai, both in the South Pacific Ocean.

Supervolcano is a term used for caldera systems that can explode in supereruptions, sending more ash and material into the air than any other type of eruption. Some volcanoes whose past eruptions have been categorized as supereruptions are Long Valley in California, Yellowstone in Wyoming, Mount Toba in Indonesia and Taupō in New Zealand.

Author's Selected Sources:

Books:
Rooney, Anne. *DK Experience: Volcano*. New York, NY: Dorling Kindersley Limited, 2006.
Rusch, Elizabeth and Susan Swan. *Volcano Rising*. Watertown, MA: Charlesbridge, 2013.

Websites:
https://earthsky.org/earth/volcanic-lightning-how-does-it-happen
https://oceanexplorer.noaa.gov/facts/volcanoes.html
https://pubs.usgs.gov/gip/volc/types.html
https://scied.ucar.edu/shortcontent/how-volcanoes-influence-climate
https://www.usgs.gov/faqs/can-earthquakes-trigger-volcanic-eruptions
https://www.usgs.gov/faqs/how-can-we-tell-when-a-volcano-will-erupt
https://www.usgs.gov/faqs/what-a-supervolcano-what-a-supereruption

Videos:
National Geographic. "Volcanoes 101." January 14, 2020. https://www.youtube.com/watch?v=VNGUdObDoLk
Khan, Sal. "Compositional and Mechanical Layers of the Earth." Khan Academy. https://www.khanacademy.org/science/cosmology-and
    -astronomy/earth-history-topic/plate-techtonics/v/compositional-and-mechanical-layers-of-the-earth
Winchcombe, Simon and Wilson, Ben. *Nova: Volatile Earth — Volcano on Fire*. WGBH and BBC Studios, 2018.

For all those waking up to their inner spark — J.K.

To Kevin and to PBP, for their inspiration and encouragement — Z.S.

ACKNOWLEDGMENTS:

A kaboom of gratitude goes out to the following individuals for fact-checking the information in this book: J. S. McNeal, MSME, instructor and PhD candidate at Portland State University, and Stephen A. Solovitz, PhD, associate professor at Washington State University Vancouver.

Published in Canada and the U.S. by Kids Can Press Ltd.
25 Dockside Drive, Toronto, ON M5A 0B5

Kids Can Press is a Corus Entertainment Inc. company

www.kidscanpress.com

The artwork in this book was rendered in ink and watercolor, and finished digitally.
The text is set in GelPen.

Edited by Kathleen Keenan
Designed by Andrew Dupuis

Printed and bound in Malaysia, in 3/2023

CM 23 0 9 8 7 6 5 4 3 2 1

LIBRARY AND ARCHIVES CANADA CATALOGUING IN PUBLICATION

Title: Kaboom! : a volcano erupts / written by Jessica Kulekjian ; illustrated by Zoe Si.
Other titles: Volcano erupts
Names: Kulekjian, Jessica, author. | Si, Zoe, illustrator.
Description: Includes bibliographical references.
Identifiers: Canadiana (print) 20220453764 | Canadiana (ebook) 20220458537 |
ISBN 9781525306495 (hardcover) | ISBN 9781525312069 (EPUB)
Subjects: LCSH: Volcanoes — Juvenile literature.
Classification: LCC QE521.3 K85 2023 | DDC j551.21 — dc23

Kids Can Press gratefully acknowledges that the land on which our office is located is the traditional territory of many nations, including the Mississaugas of the Credit, the Anishnabeg, the Chippewa, the Haudenosaunee and the Wendat peoples, and is now home to many diverse First Nations, Inuit and Métis peoples.

We thank the Government of Ontario, through Ontario Creates; the Ontario Arts Council; the Canada Council for the Arts; and the Government of Canada for supporting our publishing activity.

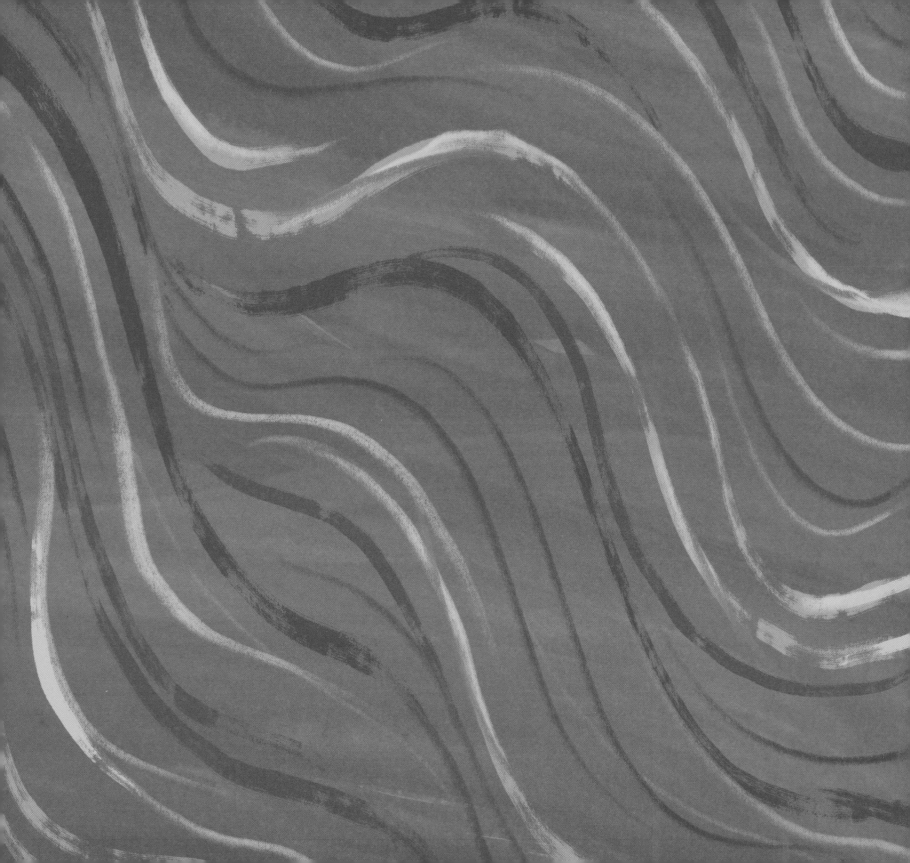